IMPERFECT ANGEL
HER JOURNEY TO WOMANHOOD

DEDICATIONS

I dedicate this book to my daughter Jalila Lorielle.

I would also like to dedicate this book to all of my readers. As the author, the biggest lesson I learned writing this story, was the fact there is no such thing as a bad experience. If all else fails, you still have that lesson that you walked away from that experience with. Knowledge makes you mentally immortal as it is something no one can take away. I hope by the end of this book, I have helped at least one person understand that you are not alone. Life is not an option; it is a blessing. Even on the worst day of your life, remember no one is perfect so there is always someone, somewhere just as imperfect as you.

Prologue

I have always been a thinker
Lately these feelings have grown deeper
It is something like an intuition
I must release this tension
As something within is the urge
No longer will it be submerged
I must follow that inner emotion
That is what it's there for
But the voices, they surround me
Claiming to put logic into destiny
With all the constant complaining
I had to reply
Logic cannot explain love
It is more complex than you think of
It is somehow the guidance
Sent from the Almighty Highness
In the most important situations
Love sometimes has no explanation
Love had me questioning myself
Maybe it is my past that I have never left
Maybe it is just parts of me that need changing
Priorities needing rearranging
All I ever wanted was to be understood
But learned that not everyone could
Understand me
I cannot let that dictate the person I am
But I need release
I may explode being filled with commotion
I must create my own voice
So I turned to my poetry
It has been mentally healthy

Instead of holding pain inside constantly
As this ink flows, my heart becomes less heavy
No matter the delivery
It has become my therapy
Whether confidential or let free
Writing or listening to spoken word
From week to week
I want to learn, listen and see
In hopes that my words are just as relating
Even though I am not the performer type
Hopefully mine is just as entertaining
I am no teacher
But write to be educational
I am no preacher
But write to be inspirational
Even though I may make it my own
It can also be another one's song
So I am regaining my happiness
Redirecting my purpose
By creating my own process
In this very moment
To share from my focus
The story of a girl to a woman
Through the effect that love
Has upon her
From my perspective to yours

The way I feel...

Share my thoughts
Spread the words of life
Love and educate those
That feels alone
The lost souls
Like a songbird
I write from within
I make their songs my own
Some, we may have in common
Others I just empathize
Though they seem so far from home
From the love and the pain
That last too long
I realize experience
Is the ultimate key
It opens our minds
To face the reality
To learn right by doing wrong
As my thoughts transfer
Through the ink to the paper
It becomes history
Once the flesh is dead and gone
Legendary it will become
Through the feelings
And through the wisdom
It may carry
Pain is a legacy
On its own
In which we are shown
So through the power of my tongue
I share my words of wisdom
In hopes to reach them
Open hearts

To the endless possibilities
That can be releasing
As the words flow
Creating the lanes of life
As our emotions let go
It makes one limitless
Beyond the core
To connect through the heart
Leaving the ear wanting more
Bringing us together
Through each other's testimonies
Letting one's voice become our own
Spoken word is now known

LOVE OF SELF

Childhood Pains

As a child, my everyday life was complicated
As extended family made me feel allocated
I cannot say I know why
But from the stories that were negotiated
The maternal side did not care for my father
Since I was a product of him
They did not want to be bothered
On the other hand
The paternal side I could not understand
I barely knew any
Blamed my father and his sinning
As the streets consumed him
Friends over family were plenty
So in our home with mother and brothers
And a father gone bad
I just decided to keep it safe
I developed the mindset we were all we had
But that did not feel like enough
Found myself still reaching for family love
Just to end up hurt again
That feeling of being unwanted
Made me feel damaged within
It was that very feeling of being unwanted
That tempted me to flaunt it
Hoping to see change and prove it wrong
But all I received in return
More experiences proving it right
So that's when I began to write
I started my writing therapy in high school
After all that heartbreak I went through
It was my tunnel out from the pain within

From putting myself in denial over and over again
Not realizing the type of people I was reaching for
Being in their presence
Created negativity and judgments one could not ignore
Constant cold-hearted gossiping
That would hurt me down to the core
Could not embrace the few positive family members
From what the others did that left my heart scorned
Then I realized they were just torn
So developed in their flaws
They only knew to come first with claws
Of anger and jealousy
When there was no real reason to envy
I wanted to forgive
But I did not know how
So I had to learn to love myself
Because at the end of the day
I really just wanted to be loved like anyone else

The way I felt...

When it rains, it pours
I've fallen so hard
On life's concrete floor
I'm tired
No fight in me left
Just want to give up
Thoughts to take my last breath
I've given away everything inside me
Until there was nothing for self
I'm awake in death
All my life I've said "yes"
Figured if I ever fall
Or fail at my best
I'd be saved, no worries
To my surprise, different story
Confused about my vision
The way it became so blurry
I'm obviously failing my test
It's burning so bad
As my heart melts
I sit, elbow to table
My forehead resting in my hand
Thinking to myself
How did it all become so difficult?
The same life experiences I swore were so simple
Are the same ones now helping my ink flow
I'm at written therapy's best
With all this hurt and pain inside
My brain needs CPR
My esteem needs a miracle
I'm trying to stay guided
Without becoming stereotypical
But it's hard

So I tell myself
This time trying is not good enough
I have to pull through
Despite loss of love and trust
So when the sun shines again
And my strides get longer
I can realize all that didn't kill me
Only made me stronger

Stop Expecting & Start Accepting

As I grew older into my mid-teens
Being accepted by anyone did not mean anything
Family or not
It was no longer important
Too many other situations I was sorting
I became more intrigued with religion
Partly feeling it was a tainted vision
But having a higher power outside of flesh
Gave me hope
During the hardships of life's tests
Experiencing personal revelations
I was facing new temptations
At the age of bodily complications
With all the societal implications
That only added to my inner frustration
With my back against the wall
Back to faith I would always fall
As the evil in my life became exposed
Including the parts of my mind it imposed
It motivated me to become mentally clear
If I truly wanted the confusion to disappear
And make way for me to continue on my journey
I may have wanted love
But I no longer needed it
My mind was finally getting some clarity
My patience for hurt was exceeded
So finally, my self-love had superseded

The way I felt...

So much anger I hold inside
Before I knew what anger really was
Reaching out for love
When I do not know what it consists of
I may be young and naive
But even a blind man can see
That I am truly in need
Of understanding
Who, what, where can I rely
To develop this true happiness inside
I take responsibility
The fact no one will save me
Overlook me as if I'm crazy
To dare try to join their family
I have had and I have lost
I learned to have
There is a cost
Too expensive for my taste
So I am lost
Lost for words to explain
Loss of energy to maintain
I am trying
Trying to keep from going insane
Trying to mask this daily growing pain
Actions outside of myself
It's easier to blame someone else
For such minimal confidence I have left
From the way they tease and taunt me
Bringing me down to their level
Where they want me
I try to stand in self honor
My sins
I commit in self-defense

This is not me
To have so much harmful intent
But I must show
What I mean, what I go through
It may be best to just let it go
So I will focus on myself
Being happy within
Since this is the only decision I have left

Placing Blame

I was making a break-through
I was finally facing the truth
The residents of my household
Would be the only family I knew
Being oblivious to the tag-teaming nights
Vows breaking as each moment passed
Came the split of my parents
Losing the last of a family that I had
It felt more and more I was alone
In a world that did not take my mother long
To go her separate way
On top of it being Christmas day
My heart was pierced in the worst way
As days turned to weeks then to months
My mother had someone new
I forced myself to put a smile on the front
When my heart was still facing the truth
My best friend was gone
And everyone just moved on
I could not take it anymore
I placed blame on my mother
Because she closed that door
On our family
I was unaware of her unhappiness
I became ungrateful of her
Instead of seeing the "S" upon her chest
My respect for her became less
With my father turned to the streets
It left only her to care how we eat
As she worked day and night
For the lives of my brothers

Just to live in places with gangs out of sight
Places where crime level was low
With schools that education would show
But the inferior feelings consumed me
I could not see the good in it
Being alone was all I could see
There I was back to prayer
Blinded with feelings
No open mind to share
I was scared
My faith was all I had to keep my sanity
I needed to let go of this situation
But my heart refused to just let it be

The way I felt...

I have to stop running from all that I have seen
I have reached the deepest sacrifice
To not allow my self-love to intervene
I stand too tall to feel so low
I work too hard to feel so
Broken on the inside
I keep telling myself
No one can judge me but God
And I am tired of living selfishly which is fraud
Of Me
I must grow up
Stop using excuses that are useless
Still hoping
Instead of knowing
Blessings will show up
Maybe no one will ever relate to me
I have generated surroundings only
Of people that develops hate in me
I have been crumbling lately
I am left with only myself
Though I try to react more sedately
I truly feel I don't have anyone else

So I am coming to you Lord
I surrender to this war
Day and night
I come as humble as I can
Only you can show me which path is right
I am ready to take that stand
Then comes the devil
With his every word sounding right
"The people who hurt you are working for me
Do my work and you can live your life worry free"

I replied, "You can get thee behind me Satan
I'm pulling through all of my struggles
The best thing I have learned through my faith
There is no need to worry about any troubles
I claim love, family and wisdom
To be brought upon my heart
Instead of negativity, lies and deceit
That you placed there from the start"

No more voices were heard
My armor had come
I am now a saved woman
I am blessed in His name
And I may have a past that has built who I am today
But I have learned many lessons
Some the hard way
There is no shame in my testimony
I have grown spiritually and emotionally
God already had this vision and I had to see it from his angle
So I now realize that I am
An imperfect angel

Fatherless Times

I cannot help the fact that I was a daddy's girl
Received negativity from all around my world
Like I chose this man
I knew he was not perfect
A wreck
Losing his self-respect
All I did was protect
I gave excuses
Even if it was foolish
I had to defend his honor
The minimal dignity he had left
Even though I began seeing him less
My soul could not rest
I had to put our love to the test
Because maybe when he saw me depressed
He would change his quest
Get his addictions addressed
Even if it was just for my request
But I no longer knew the man he turned into
Then came the arrest
I was so hurt and disappointed
Then my brother convinced me it was best
I must admit it was too much to digest
So every day I would stress
At least he was still alive
I guess he made it through his tests
But there were many more to come
I felt so useless
As my father had more love for the streets
How could he be so ruthless?
So concerned with his coolness

The family labeled him as a nuisance
I was betrayed
Thinking maybe I should have taken that trade
When my mother offered
The best friend to me he portrayed
It started to fade
Our relationship strayed
It took damn near a decade
For me to realize that this monster he displayed
Was there to stay
I was so hurt and afraid
I just prayed and prayed
As I watched this renegade
Hoping that at least God could persuade
This man to clean this mess he had made
Because I was broken

The way I felt...

There was a time
That you felt so near to me
Everything was so clear
Now nothing but fear in me
You are so far away

Though you are here in the flesh
Your mind is slowly fading away
The love you claim in my regard
Is starting to put me in an area of grey

Unconsciously I hurt
Full of resentful pain
Because you left me all alone
To face this cruel world
As your promises went astray

Where are you
When my heart gets broken
Or my security is stolen
I had to learn to live without you
Build a world of becoming a woman around you

Making twice as many mistakes
Putting my well-being at stake
Just to overcome being afraid
And to one day forgive you
So my emotions no longer lie in the way

One thing you have taught me
When my face is to the dirt
The strength to endure
No longer will I hurt

No matter what you decide to do
Or how many times you desert
I will be alright

Time has shown me
Love can come differently
You changed on me
Your broken promises
Living in my heart rent-free
Now I just depend on serenity

There was a time
That you felt so near to me
Everything was so clear
Now there's even more strength in me
By you now being so far away

On My Own

For a long time
I did not understand
My parents' divorce or life
Our family was supposed to withstand
No matter the hardships or sacrifice
But I guess God had his own plan
While everyone moved on
I was too young to realize
There was pain that love could not fix
My oldest brother was tired of it
He packed his stuff one day and left
After some huge argument
Despite the promises not kept
Being the closest to a father I had
Now I was down to Mom, other brother and self
No one to educate me on life and men
Our brick home was turning to sand
It was all taking over my mind
Made me weaker by the day
I would just sit in the window
Plotting solutions, I intend to
Use to release the hurt and resentment
I had toward my mother for leaving
Toward my brother for his lack of commitment
Ultimately for my dad for the abandonment
Everyone was so far away
After suicidal thoughts
I realized I was truly lost
The ones I needed most
For guidance and security
And anything else I needed to know

Were gone
There I was alone
I needed to get back on my journey to womanhood
Just now it was all on my own

The way I felt...

I never thought I would be here in this place
Full of deception
Not knowing what is real anymore
I don't know how to feel anymore
Facing the interjections
That I have allowed in my life
Leaving me with myself
So vulnerable to the strife
Over and over again
I have let it come in
No more depending
Felt alone from the beginning
Only God knows when my story ends
So I have nothing left to be lending
Some will think I have become condescending
I am only being truthful
I have been so caught up in everyone around me
Selfless and becoming my own enemy
Seems like the drama has filled my surroundings
So I will spend my time on more profound things
Dedicating the energy, I have been left with
To all the personal goals
Become more selfish
It used to seem this was the last place I wanted to be
As it only seemed to be dark and lonely
But it is more than what I think I see
The less distraction
The more quality in life I believe
So it is meaningful to be on my own
More challenges make me stronger
Learning more about myself than I have ever known
Sometimes I speak to the sky
To give thanks to the Most High

For showing me no matter where I am
It will never just be me, myself and I

Immature State of Mind

As time went on I matured
Not saying my pain was cured
But life was getting better
My father eventually got his life together
Becoming sober and maintaining a healthy relationship
I was happy the way my dad was seeking happiness
It was in the right way
A lot had changed in our closeness
But that is not always a bad thing
I realized it was not my job to change anyone
Through prayer God always got it done
I knew deep down inside
I will forever be Daddy's girl
Now I was in my own world
I wish I forgave my family first
To try and break this generational curse
Of being self-centered
As I thought being there for my family
Would make people be there for me
But when tables turned
I felt I was always ending up alone
I decided to separate from them emotionally
In order to focus on my own opportunities
I just wanted them to know
Their behavior did show
I saw the way I was treated
Even through the battles I defeated
Love was damaging me
The only love I knew was supposed to come from family
And I loved them all unconditionally
But they did not pay attention

To know what it was I truly needed
I was too young to let my journey for love finish
I did not think how the lack of love in the beginning
Would affect the way I reached for love in the ending

The way I felt...

I was always there for you
But you are not here for me
There are trials I go through
Though I have been warned
That this will become you
I denied that truth
I would not dream
This day coming into place
Now I am being slapped with a clean reality check
Right in my face
The signs were there
Red flags I neglected
Because my own beliefs felt more protected
That this was a two-way street
I help you
You help me
But you left me lying in deceit
So know that trail you walk is not perfect
Another one of your tribulations will surface
And I'll remember this moment
Left alone with my wounds still open
As if I was not worth it
Then I will leave you in your pity of self
For a purpose
To feel the anguish I felt
Two wrongs
Do not make it right
But how else will you learn
If whenever you're blind, I become your sight
Then when I am blinded
You carry on and pay it no mind
My hurt is always mine all alone
Though my biggest lesson

The strength it dwells inside of me
That I can prosper with or with out
Any person that contributed to this discovery
My life is mine to hold
You did what your heart told
So I took that negative energy
That overpowered me for so long
Changed it into ambition
In order to forgive you and move on

The way I felt... (deeper)

The wheels are steady spinning
The ending is beginning
I'm so lost in this puzzle
So many pieces are missing
I took all that I can take
Until there was no more peace to make
I'm flooded in the desire of revenge
I fight myself
As my teeth clench
This is an unchosen battle
Can I ever win?
How does love go so sour?
I am always by myself in the end

There is no patience left
The fire is in my eyes
Even I am so surprised
How did it get to this?
They did not walk in my shoes
I feel so used and abused
I know these feelings are of the devil
Yet mine are at an unbearable level
So where is God now?
He will never forsake me
Yet He has let Satan take me
See there I go again
Blaming another for my sins
Screaming why me
Instead of letting God show his peace
I do not understand
Why I'm so angry at man
I've lost my faith in God's hands
To flesh and its plans

Release...
I must forgive and let it go
Amazingly God has taken His control
Back into my life and my soul
As Satan knew all along
But I didn't really know
So Satan placed burdens more and more
He may have won that battle
But not the war
Because I never lost all faith
And God never let me go
He forgave me
He held me
I realized he never left me
He just taught me
So next time I will know

Is Blood Thicker Than Water?

As I was distancing myself
My uncommitted feelings soon went left
Because I was right back to feeling ashamed
As this was not me
Just a pack of wolves around me
And I was the only sheep
It was taking too much of my energy
Manually forcing myself to be like them
I decided
To no longer live in this contempt
So in my late teens, I branched off
To find my own place in the world at any cost
I wanted to find my own way
Taking the lessons learned from the past
Putting that want for love in a far enough place
Deep within my heart
So the next heartless person that comes around
I could pin point that waste of time from the start
I was growing out of that darkness
I was letting the past be the past
Focusing on love for myself
As that seemed the only love that would last
I learned many things about me
Being the only girl and youngest of my siblings
I developed some spoiled ways
But I learned to humble myself on the rainy days
Put my foot down when my worth is tested
There were pros and cons to having brothers
That was actually invested
Like informing me on men
When there was no dad

The type of person I was
Sometimes I did what they said
Other times I did what I wanted just because
I thought it was best
Now that I was accepting things for what they were
I had to learn to pass those old tests
In order to continue with life
Moving on from the negativity
That was creating sleepless nights
I became involved with my friends
As we all were running from problems
We became each other's cleanse
No bloodline joined us
But our love grew stronger
Primarily through our trust
And we all knew
Starting refreshed and new was a must
It was time for all of us to mentally grow up
Stealing control of my life like it was a crime
I was in an ending and beginning
All at the same time
Ending the part of me
That let others dictate my happiness
But beginning the new me
With the love of myself being the first to address

The way I felt...

Nothing comes between the connections we share
Running through the valley of the unknown
Depending on one another as if no one else cares
Actually just misunderstood
But we somehow understand each other
Living our lives on the edge
Never noticing the cliff is so deep
Yet we protect each other
Falling is no option
Facing the secrets we keep
This jungle of lust
It has captivated us
Knocked us into the dust
Breaks us down time after time
We continue to try new things
It is the constant flow of adrenaline
That keeps us coming back like an addiction
We all know better in most cases
But we need to explore
Weaving through these situations
Feeling the need to want more
The united force we hold
Unbreakable to most
Learning through one another
Sharing moments no one else knows
Just us
Built a bond of infinite trust
No regrets
Stories that we will never forget
The disobedience we all have
Do not seem half as bad
Until we reflect
Then we realize we make certain decisions

Not caring what anyone says
We have our own tunnel visions
There are times we let emotions guide us
We fight and argue
Then convince each other the past is behind us
It is the way we breakthrough
It makes our bond even deeper
When we grow up and apart
The experiences will become teasers
As we laugh at the mere thought of our actions
It will make the humiliation become easier
Blaming the fact of age on our many mistakes we unfold
In reality it is our part of growing up
Into women, from being these rebellious souls

Finding Me

It was time to go college
No time for books
As friends were all that I acknowledged
I thought I could do it all
Long fun nights to last minute homework
Until my grades began to fall
I went from Dean's list recognition
To dance team auditions
Then distractions that pushed me to transition
To losing sight of my true mission
I graduated high school early
Because I did not have time to be girly
But now I cared
I wanted the beautiful long hair
Painted covered skin with Asian created nails
Trendy material things
Just so someone would notice me
Including the fact
It was what the media said was pretty
I just wanted to feel sexy
But that did not last long
It was not my personality
I barely knew what love was anymore
Whether relationship or friendship
I silently screamed for more
My mind was on myself
Since I was all I had left
I did not let my mind be consumed with anyone else
I went from selfless to selfish
In one huge step
I knew the real prize was within me

Then I looked at the men and friends I began choosing
The ones that neglected to see the love I had inside
They were the real ones losing
I was not perfect
But I loved myself flaws and all

The way I felt...

I used to want the "pretty" yellow skin tone
The "perfect" small physique
I never realized
I was already perfectly unique
See the physical does not define me
Yet
I let norms of society confine me
As if
My brown darker skin tone
My larger bust and waist
My natural rooted hair
Will not be pursued upon
But
My parents always told me
Beauty is only skin deep
I beg to differ
As I hold beauty down to my soul
As a young child
I never knew that I hold
Though
Life was never perfect
It was always very real
Watching the "perfect" women on TV
The more out of place I'd feel
Because I was far from that
Quite opposite
As a matter of fact
I was not happy with myself
Pretending with everyone else
Masked smiles
Until no smiles were left
Then God showed me
I was made this way on purpose

As his own individual creation
Not a figure of imagination
But by Him
No matter if I have locks or weave
If my hair is down to my knees
If I have perfect straight teeth
If the ideal measurements I meet
I am made of God's image
Though my self-esteem can be timid
Feeling too tall, but not thin
I am too dark, all over my skin
I can go on forever complaining
But I would rather
Learn to love the skin I am in
I was made this way for a reason
Because I am perfectly unique

RESPECT OF SELF

First Time

The first part was established
With learning to love myself
But the main part I was missing
Was the self-respect concept
There I was still searching
Trying to become a woman
It was urgent
Listening to my friend's sexual excursions
I realized I was still a virgin
I wanted to have sex
As it was next
In my womanhood steps
When it should have been self-respect
I had just started college
It was not that I didn't have sexual knowledge
I just chose not to acknowledge
The information that was once given
To cherish my body and prevent from sinning
I was only concerned with this unattached living
Plus, my friend's juicy stories enticed me
They always put the stories together so nicely
So I began to feel separated
When it came to sex
I always hesitated
The mere thought of someone entering my domain
Made me so devastated
But I was tired of not having the juicy gossip
It was time that I felt liberated
I always wondered why women shared stories
When a guy was surely dedicated
But failed to inform

When they were being under appreciated
Back to losing my virginity
It was a big experience
It was my young girl clearance
That was mixed with my selfish adherence
Together made me feel ready
I believed this would transform me into womanhood
Then I met him
I was ready to have my first time
I had just met this guy
But he had me on cloud nine
As he spoke all the right lines
Then the opportunity came
In that split second I made up my mind
It was definitely time

The way I felt...

What am I thinking?
Am I ready for this adventure?
My body is full of nerves and tension
It is way easier said than done
My heart is racing at the speed of light
There is no turning back
Then he will no longer love me
And the humiliation of our friends
Oh Lord! Please help me!
This man and his body looking all sexy
As he kisses my neck
I can no longer distract myself
I fall into the moment
I do not want anyone else
But him

The tension runs so deep
As he makes me feel so good
I close my eyes and drift to dream
As my anxiety starts to lower
As he starts to undress me
I start to get a cold shoulder
The dream is now reality
As his fingertips glide my body
With no direction nor formality
He takes me away into a fantasy
As he kisses up my body
To my lips
Then slides his manhood between my hips
As he tells me to breathe
I exhale until I feel the tip
I jump and slide up

He sees that I'm hesitating to face this pain
So he begins to lick down my stomach
Until he reaches my womanly plain
Between my thighs as they tense
From the sensation his tongue moves sent
As he kisses and sucks my juices away
I vibrate with an arched back
As my legs start to shake
Now I am wet as the ocean
As he climbs back up
Looking me deep in the eyes
As he slides into me, he speeds up

After a couple slow penetrations
It starts to feel better
Becoming my new addiction I'm creating
Non-verbal communicating
Just the moans of our nature
We were in
I love the way he caters
With every movement
As we grind towards ecstasy
Giving him all that is left in me

His groans as he release
Begin disconnecting me
As I was not warned of this part
Then he comes back to reality
From his seconds of exploding ecstasy
And just kisses me
Passionately
More passionate than ever before
I have given the best part of me to this man
And that excitement
Only makes me yearn for him more

Next thing I know I am coming a river
From the full thrust as he penetrates my center
I begin to quiver
As his acceleration drives me crazy
Even more when it becomes steady
My body elated from our special night
At this moment life feels so right
As he lay beside me and holds me tight
I close my eyes
Knowing I will forever remember this very night

Not Love

After that night
Everything was the same in life
I did not feel more like a woman
I just ended up catching more feelings for him
For such an important moment of life
It was over before the blink of an eye
But my heart took flight
As cliché as it may sound
I felt warm in his arms
Comfort and safety in his presence
I felt he meant no harm
When actually, I should have stayed alarmed
Instead I became infatuated
Until my fantasy was castrated
When it was time for his feelings to be demonstrated
In the beginning
It felt like we were on the same mission
But he had other intentions
That was taking his attention
I would be with him every night
When it was time to leave
I always put up a fight
Because I was seeing him less and less
I was feeling used
By a man that has lost his interest
So I kept allowing him to do it
Until I could not take it anymore
Being his night lover
Then come morning my heart was sore
It just felt so good
When he had his way with me

But the real downfall started
With his love for the streets
Leaving me regretting that he took my virginity
But that was something too late to consider
Since I didn't, I was slowly becoming bitter
Asking myself questions
Like, why this was not sacred to him?
Why I was not good enough?
It seemed not as serious for most men
As I heard the stories of my friends
So I eventually let out my heart to him
He just apologized for not willing to change
Even though a great friendship remained
I knew my love for him would never be the same
Plus, it was so stupid of me
Immaturity did not let me think of pregnancy
Possibilities of affecting my future goals
Even contracting an STD
I knew condoms did not protect from everything
Like the heartbreak if he became typical
Only wanting the sex
Then never hearing from him
Or when my heart became an issue
I knew he was not that stereotypical
Outside of my feelings for him
Being his friend first
Made him pretty predictable
I just did not understand
I wanted this man
To have as my own
My feelings were strong
While he only wanted street royalty
It did not matter about my loyalty
He had other plans of his own

Thankfully
He at least kept his honesty
Instead of leading me on
That truth did hurt
But helped me realize it was not love
It was only lust
So we agreed to remain friends
And to never lose touch
From that day we only grew trust
Because he was the first guy in my life
That knew respecting me was a must
For a while, friendship did not feel like enough
But eventually
It became easier to let go of
That fantasy of having his love

The way I felt...

I'm looking in your eyes
As you are watching mine
The sweet temptation
Of amazing sensations
When our clothes have disappeared
Our thoughts have been cleared
We are in a whole new world
See
You talk with a flow
That your friends don't know
It slips you deep within my soul
You have me feeling
And believing
You bring out this woman in me
That is only for you to see
Like when we are just relaxing
I still desire your sweet passion
The anticipation of you exploding
Gave passion to my exploring
Of you
As our sweat starts to drip
And I can feel your finger-tips
On all my sweetest parts
I become willing to be your ride or die chick
Or your damsel in distress
If that's the best fit
It is too much power in us dating
I think you're procrastinating
Maybe I am just infatuating
While we're playing some game
That you feel you're a player in
Now I'm feeling this is just pretend
How you have me strung out

On this constant living doubt
Of you being the one
While you are just having fun
With me
Your love is my weakness
Yet I still want to keep trying
For the love that I am seeking
From you
It's like you have me under this spell
And I can't tell
What you want from me
Love is the game of give and take
I am giving you me
Then trying to take you
Since you will not allow me
There is no love in our truth

Love vs. Lust

Following that experience
I had a more want to be intimate
I admit I was scared in the beginning
But the fear of constantly sinning
Was ending
See, first it was my family
That I did not feel loved me
Now it was the men
I was tired of this reality
So I figured out how to win the game
I was no longer going to stress my brain
Trying to understand
Why I was the only one loving me?
Instead
I stripped away my feelings
I figured I would be two steps ahead
Self-respect was so far from my head
And I was no longer thinking with my heart
Setting the physical and emotional apart
I began entertaining bad boys
It was easier to handle their noise
I knew they were not real men
Because it was never any intellect
Just pride in being direct
There was nothing they really wanted
Just an experience
So their egos could flaunt it
But I admit I became intrigued
Knowing I was way out of their league
It only made them try harder to be with me
The challenge

Of taking a man's attention from the streets
Turning it into only wanting me
It excited me to a degree
The lack of love from my ex
Made me like this, I believe
After one failed attempt too many
I learned it did not make me happy
Just because it was more easy
Going this way was a dead end street
Plus, living that way
With complete
Lack of self-respect
Was not me
My heart and feelings
I needed to protect
This way of living was not real or love
I was purely basing my happiness
Off the deceit and lust

The way I felt...

Oh, how I wish
You would have your way with me
Take me into your arms slowly
Enrich me
With your full soft lips
Kiss me
With those strong smooth hands
Caress me
Share me in your destiny
Confess to me
The sexual fantasies you want to invest in me
I will give you authority over my physical being
For this one night only
Put aside feelings
Let's make love on the beach
Our bodies covered with sand
Take me away into your passion
It is getting late
As I sit on the passenger side of your front seat
Squeezing my knees together so hard from the heat
Dwelling deep inside of me
From the desire to have you sexually
From your head to your feet
I want to test everything I have been yearning
My only concern is
Are you ready?
To give in to this temptation
Then cherish every given sensation
As we embark on this exploration
I will be your sex slave
Make home on your manly plantation
As you
Slide into my waterfall

And it splashes onto your ship
Handle my current
As you work towards the shore
The more I moan to have more
The more you seem to have in store
Towards our journey to ecstasy
If only you will connect with me
Sexually
Don't let me go
But you must
Because one more minute this close to you
I am bound to continue
Giving in to our lust

Growing Pains

If I was not showing the love and respect in self
How could I expect either one from anyone else?
That was when I knew
I was not learning the real lesson
That it is alright to be alone
I was still reaching for unwanted love
Instead of being happy on my own
So I decided to reach out to my friends
Since with them I never had to pretend
Get some solid advice
On what a real woman is like
But that was no help
They were mirror images
As each were crossing their own bridges
Into womanhood

The way I felt...

Love will never be reciprocated
If love within thy self is not first generated
Soul searching doesn't come by nature
As entitlement of a woman doesn't come with an age
But of mental ability
Not any sexual capability
But to take heed to life lessons
As experience is the key
To unlock your true torch
To ignite your self-worth
How much do you really mean to yourself?
So many characteristics unseen
Like secrets that are kept
The love that you express
Cannot be confused with sex
Because then you will be quick to retaliate
With blurred vision into accepting less
Than what you deserve
You have to learn yourself and love yourself
There is wisdom in these words
As I reflect on my mistakes
It is wisdom I wish I would have heard
Instead I did what I preferred
So you must know you are worth more
Even starting from the floor
Just stand tall
Remember the worth you are fighting for
You are queens
Put your desire into unknown knowledge
Despite what your peers do
Just always remember
It all starts within
Deciding to lose or win

It all determines when
You grow from a girl to a woman

Love is Blind

I was only twenty years old
What could I have known about true love?
My friends and I heard the same speech growing up
To cherish our bodies and not quickly give it up
That meant sexually and emotionally
Until marriage of course
But it was too late for that
It was so easy to try and
Force ourselves
To look at men for what we wanted them to be
We were victims to social beliefs
That once we united sexually
The next step was matrimony
Because then we add attachments
Since we gave our bodies
Our hearts followed aimlessly
But men sometimes move shamelessly
Not thinking where the end could be
They could have sexual relations
And still have nothing invested
So that was when I started to believe
If he wanted the relationship of monogamy
He would have made me his wife
In the beginning
Just another struggle of a woman
When she becomes blinded
By love

The way I felt...

Men have no idea
Cannot start to understand
The magnitude of being a woman

God made no mistakes
When he removed that rib from men
To create the constitution of a woman

It is amazing
Our bodies create something from nothing
Bringing life
Only the substance of being a woman

Each of us were brought into this world
By women that took that stand
Knowing the significance of being a woman

Each soul is unique
Yet shares the strength of women's fruitful grain
The ultimate complexity of being a woman

It takes courage of dare
To nurture, love and defend
The essentialities of being a woman

No one can doubt
Nor begin to try to question
The true caliber of being a woman

When you are blessed with the beauty
Of which ever woman you are within
Embrace the element of being that woman

True Friends

Spending time with my main circle of friends
I became more open
But it was not to men
It was to help them
See, when it came to my friends
I was always the tie of loose ends
We were all so different
When it came to life decisions
I was the glue that stuck everyone together
While constituting all the group events
I would always settle the drama
That ever stirred up between us
My kindness has always been my weakness
Because I had too much
My friends and I always had adventures
Little did we know
Our outgoing, spoiled, "thinking we know everything" mindsets
Even though they were all different
Started our roller coasters
We rode on daily
On our own individual journeys
To gaining maturity
And becoming real women
Even though we were in our prime
We were living fast in time
Creating memories to adore
While still knocking at Satan's door
As we faced some hard decisions
We wanted to try everything
Just to say it was nothing we were missing
So when we grew older

We could say we did it all
Together we stood so tall
Before we walked as women
We had plenty of time to crawl
And go through our falls
To really learn what life was all about
I admired each of my friends
For their own individual reasons
Most of all because they were not there for a season
They were there for a lifetime
It was not about the friendships
That was created before anyone else
In our world
It was all about the friends that came and never left
It was just us
Each friend and I had our own story
None of which were boring
All of them inspired me
As I continued on my own journey

The way I felt...

Life lessons are never brought easy
But we learn
We live
No regrets
You teach me
As I hope I teach you
The bond that we hold
It is truly unconditional
Whatever the world does to break us
When our young-minded decisions are reckless
We face it together
Generating unforgettable memories

From the day that I met you
We had instant common grounds
We were soft petal roses
Searching for the answers
To where our path goes
We have always been on the same page
In our own separate novels of life
I grow with you
I learn about you
Yet sometimes I feel I never know you
But I trust you somehow
Despite our naive hearts
Which the flesh of men takeover
Through temptation as sin
I see your unique intelligence
This wicked road of those demons we travel will end
When we overcome that mental habit
And become emotionally sober

We met at a state of very young

When we felt there was so much time
In life, before the true women we'd become
The cover to our book
Express so many different values
Of the chapters inside
Lost souls searching for answers
For love
For family unknown of
God brought us together for his own special purpose
Years of fight, hurt and pain
We need each other to regain
Our life's purpose

Though we travel on different journeys
I would detour across the world
If you were to get lost
Because you are my friend
No matter if we fight
Lose our trust
If we might
Our love will stay mutual
Nothing can take away the things we have been through
As butterflies we have broken out of our cocoons
Into this real world
As we find love
No matter how far we go
I know we will be together on a spiritual scale
Because we hold a piece of each other
In ourselves

Mischievous Behavior

Starting college together
We held strong to each other
That exciting feeling of being away from home
Did not last that long
We became bored
We felt far from existence
Coming from city life
To seeing only fields in the distance
We needed to fill our spare time
What else were better decoys?
Than road trips and boys
Being on a college campus
With limited places to go
You tend to see the same people everywhere
From class to your dorm room floor
So we began internet dating
As college fun was fading
We were desperate for excitement
Looking for options with the most enticement
But without the emotional distraction
A world purely off of physical attraction
We were meeting so many different types
Of men, well boys that we liked
It was starting to be a game we were playing
It was making our dating life simple
Because it did not matter what we were saying
It was not face to face with them
Some guys lived in faraway places
This left the truth lost in cyber space
But I had a plan
I wanted to find a man

That loved me for me
So I decided the only way to do that
Was to always give honesty
Just being myself
Then everything changed
When I came across his page
I was intrigued by him
He gave me a chill through my limbs
From his sexy profile pictures
To thoughtful messages he would send
I was talking to him day and night
Connecting on levels beyond sight
It turned into us deciding to be together
I never had a long-distance relationship
But I was ready to try
He had me feeling he was the one
With our limit to the sky
Until I became tired of the mystery
That at one moment attracted me
Since he was my one and only
I felt it was time for us to meet
After months of conversations about it
I learned, that he was not for me
Hundreds of excuses
That he gave constantly
It was like he wanted to remain unseen
Then I realized our bond was not real
As people can be who they want on a computer screen
Especially when you live across the country
So I concluded online dating was not for me
I was being real to find real love
But it did not mean anything
After all the months of life wasted
I decided to no longer chase it

I had no more hope stored
Back to point A in the love category
Back to the drawing board

The way I felt...

The things we will do
To have someone to call our own
Not sure if he has to be worth it
Showing him love whether or not he deserves it

At first we are so blinded
By the need to be wanted
That we lose the truth
In the real ways we want it

Standards have been thrown out the window
That the relationship should hold
Not thinking of the future
Will only let temptation and lust unfold

Not knowing of true love
So the false one becomes enough
It is better than not having love at all
If we have a love that is tough

Unintentional lies to family
Friendships starting to end
Scared of change or losing him
He becomes worth more than family or friends

Then the point of losing self
When we realize we have become someone else
The image in the mirror appears blurred
As that initial bliss has slowly gone left

Remembering the lonely moments
Makes you vow to never be alone
Scared of another failed relationship

So you create some type of right in his wrong

Then the last few people in your life
That did not give up on you for changing
Convince you to focus on your happiness instead
So you start feeling, being single may not be that bad

You finally become fed up and leave another one behind
Then you meet another one
He puts all the right things into your mind
Then you are back at square one

Revolving cycle that goes in circles
Never learning
Blaming everything else instead of yourself
For your own mistakes returning

Like moving too fast
Not taking time to see his intentions
Getting to know this man flaws and all
Forgetting a relationship cannot walk
If no one takes the time to let it crawl

Until we realize that purpose
We will never understand
Just keep creating bad experiences
As we keep convincing ourselves all we want is a man

Mischievous Behavior (continued)

I started to become this selfish monster
Heartless to love disaster
I faced many more hardships
Because my self-respect was not a part of it
Spending all my time with my friends of the same
We began dealing with so many men
It was a full-time job just to remember their names
We felt the more we entertained
The furthest we were from love's pain
So we ran the streets
Constantly
I loved myself too much
I could not think to love anyone else
My heart and mind was so out of touch
As I did not have enough left
Endurance for my pain to worsen
By another person
I needed to be in control
I could not take being hurt anymore
The endless nights
And senseless fights
With other women
About some guy that sang them the same song
When neither one of us could even call him our own
That was when it hit me
That all the important things in my life
Was all going downhill quickly
My plate felt so full
But it was actually closer to becoming empty

The way I felt...

I am not physically blind
Yet still I cannot see
It's like driving with the sun
Glaring through the windshield
With no visor
I cruise aimlessly
Where am I going?
Unwilling to stop
My sense of direction compromised
I am depending on a lot
Should I keep going?
Change my life's plot
I'm going back and forth with myself
I believe I'm so close
Too close
I can reach out my hand
And touch it
That close
So much going on in my life
I'm just trying not to waste it
But I'm slowly eating myself inside out
The longer I try to fake it
I have a monster deep inside me
And I tried not to wake it

Too late

I was created for a purpose
Living on the edge, I'm so nervous
Trying to learn my responsibility
In providing God's service
But it is the failure I protest
The destination is success

I see no other route there
Arriving with integrity have become rare
I feel there's no sense in complaining
I was told life isn't fair
By many means
I will rise to this place
Long journey coming
But I know
It's where I belong
I will not let myself give up
Despite the moment of hesitation
I will pick back up each and every time
With my self-aspiration

A Turn for the Worse

As time went on
My friends and I grew apart
Our similar pasts held us together
But we were all experiencing new starts
It was the summer after sophomore year
I received a letter from the college I was attending
Advising me I owed thousands
Prior to registering for any more classes
I decided to work all summer
So my days got longer
Leaving no time for fun
I was back living with my mom
By the end of the summer
I still did not have enough
I needed to figure out my next move
Living under my mother's roof
With all her criticism and rules
I needed someone to vent to
I was out one night when I met someone new
Man this guy was so smooth
After a few months
He convinced me to
Move in together
I was giving this man an important part of me
Without even knowing it
Forgetting all my past testimonies
At the time
It was the only way out it seemed
Plus, he was giving me the love I yearned for
After losing my dad to the streets
Things were perfect for a moment

Until one night I got into an argument
Some drunken girl testing my patience
And this man lost it
As she tried to throw her fist my way
He slapped her right across her face
She just fell to the ground
I was without movement or sound
As he continued to kick her continuously
I was in shock but proud
I felt safe with him now
Refusing to see that red flag
If he would do that to this woman
What he would do to me when I made him mad
Then one night I was able to see
Coming in after a night of fun with my girls
He began searching through my phone
He saw a number that a friend dialed on her own
He called it back to hear a deep voice
Instantly broke my phone in half
I jumped out of the shower body still moist
Trying to explain my case
Not a full sentence left my mouth
Before his hand slammed hard into my face
I was hurting inside and out
I just began crying out loud
Until he charged out of the house
I jumped up
Immediately packed my things
Then started searching for my purse and keys
Until I realized my wallet was missing
So I just ran out to my car
To find out it would not start
There was no telling what he did with the parts
So I sat and thought of where to go

As any family or friends lived too far
So I rushed to a neighbor's door
Begging to use their phone
I could barely talk
Trying to explain what just went on
As he came behind me in the hall
And grabbed me by my hair
To try and make me fall
Telling me to scream if I dared
As he dragged me through our door
I crawled into a ball in the center of the floor
Praying he did not kill me
He made threats he would if I ever tried leaving
I was truly held captive
Until one day on my way to work
I detoured to safety
Scared to tell anyone the truth
From the threats he made to me
I just found my own place
Pretending
A mutual split was the case
I moved on with my life just like that
I focused on moving forward and never looked back

The way I felt...

I found love
Or so I thought
I was intrigued by what I wanted you to be
That the true you
I was unable to see
As I gave you the best of me
Until there was nothing left of me
And I have lost whatever rest of me
Into you
Have I given you this control?
Or have you stolen my soul
With your lies
And promises that seem so real
Heartache wasn't part of the deal

Were you ever willing to love me?
Since you captured me
Expressed the true love
That you knew was only temporary
And had me learning that the hard way
Yet I stay
I pray
Cater to you in every way
That my mind, body and heart can
I do whatever you ask me to
But not to end like this
You are a horrible creature
The exact teacher
That I need
You opened my eyes
In ways I didn't realize
That had me making excuses for my heartache
I wanted your lies to be true

So much that I began believing them
I was tricking myself
That the lonely nights
The senseless fights
Were all worth it
My patience
Constantly being put to the test
By you and your ego

And the way you treat women
Should have helped make my decision
To love you
Instead I accepted all the pain you put me through
Including the wind, you knocked out of me
Not only did you lose me
I lost me too
My loved ones warned me
I should have left
But I didn't
I chose to stay in it
So I have to accept what I went through
The best thing is to learn from it
I must move on to something more
It is hard with the pain inside
That still resonates in the core
Of my heart

Someone better will come along
When you realize I am truly gone
You will come crawling back
With your same love song
That will fade out of my existence
Because far in the distance
Of my mind I will remember
I sacrificed it all for us

And your heart
That I once believed I held a piece of
I no longer care to have
I know of your mistaken love

Second Strike, You're Out

At first I agreed to move with him
Just to get out of my mom's house
But over time I learned to love him
I had faith in the future we would have had
I swear love will make you do the craziest things
Because after I moved on
He eventually found me
Then he started hounding me
Sent flowers and gifts
Millions of texts saying "I'm sorry"
Until I eventually became weak
I started remembering the beginning
How he made me happy
So I forgave him
Allowed him to come back
As my common sense was definitely off track
I did not want to be alone
I felt by overcoming these hard times
It would only make our relationship more strong
We were back dating
The good did not last too long
Even though we both had a place of our own
We shared everything else
So you could imagine how I felt
When some woman emailed me on social media
Telling me my man has just left
Her home, and since he did not inform me
She would do it herself
She began telling me everything down to how they met
The only reason she was doing this
Because she was tired of being put on the shelf

I hung up to sit and think about this information
I remembered all the nights he called to check on my location
It was really for his confirmation
So he would not get caught
That was when I realized
The only reason he accused me of being with someone else
Was because he was doing it himself
As for that woman
I hoped she knew karma is an evil wish
Even though she told me the truth
She still knew I was the one he was with
I did everything for this man
But this time was the end
I was fed-up with the heartbreak
He was causing me over and over again
I was convinced this man would break me
I was truly an emotional mess
I went back into my written therapy
Now it was at its best

The way I felt...

I trusted you
Until I busted you
In that bald-faced lie
That you told from those unfaithful lips
About all your distasteful dips
Into every woman you meet
I see monogamy you cannot keep
Do I not satisfy you?
Save those pathetic excuses for someone else
Who actually wants to listen to it
Before we really get into it
And I end with doing something I may regret
I may eventually forgive you
But never will I forget
The pain and humiliation
The ultimate lack of dedication
You have to our commitment
Though I settled for the flaws you came with
I should have seen this
Coming
You know I actually loved you
But you did not love me
Or our relationship
Just what you thought it could be
I never would have thought
That you would actually
Be uncaring and disrespectful enough
To actually get caught

With this less than woman
That believes having you
Is really considered as having something
I would like to ask her

How do you convince yourself it's worth it?
Knowing he loves his exception
Because the everyday rule
This is played by you
Is just a temporary interception
Of the life he has truly built for another
Stop denying the real truth
Then you will get the real answer
Of what you truly are
To him
You think he will give up everything for you
I doubt it
You are his experiment to see
If he "still got it"

One day you will find someone of your own
He will love every part of your existence
He will listen and hear you
Pay attention and really see you
Spend all his time with you
The time he cannot
He will spend thinking of you
As you become mesmerized by his heart
And fall in love with that man
You will have a breath of fresh air
That you have someone now that truly cares
About you and only you

Then one day everything will change
That man will slowly slip away
First the less calls day to day
Then more time spent away
Then he has less conversation to make
Even lying in the same bed
He will seem so far away

That is when it will hit
Finally, you will start to get the itch
Your woman's intuition will be lit
You'll start searching his pockets, car and phone
As your past comes to mind it will click
Your heart will start racing
As you scramble
Jealousy and guilt makes it harder
To find this woman he has been with
You cannot find anything but you know in your heart she exists
Then everything starts to make sense
I am warning you
Karma does exist

The way I felt... (deeper)

I used to think you hurt me
But in reality
You helped me
To become an even better woman for the next
And all that crying
Was just my bottled emotions becoming a little too complex
I know now I could've just relaxed and let God
I want to convince myself I was overly infatuated
And my heart was just overly captivated
So I ignored the fact I was never emotionally motivated
But I know now I could've just relaxed and let God
It didn't kill me that you turned out to be the antonym of a man
That's a strong insult so I'll let my intellect expand
To explain my reasoning so you will understand
While you were so busy being night-life gifted
I was taking our time apart to become spiritually shifted
Into the woman I needed to be, even for you
I never complained
Nor went against the grain
When it came to you and me
Versus what you do
I just supported you
They say "a strong woman walks behind a strong man"
But what if that man becomes weak?
Because he falls into the devil's streak
Of material and self
Do you let him continue to build the castle of sand?
Or walk away with the little unbroken heart you have left?
Because after all those times we would go back and forth
You gained pride as I lost self-worth
You pushing away your back bone
To go get a quick bone
That is moving so backwards

You want to be more than just an option
Yet that was not the plan you were plotting
With those actions of a coward
You always tell me what I do and say wrong
I appreciate the honesty when it comes
The constructive criticism where it belongs
But I accepted your flaws
You continuously belittled mine
Instead of realizing you had a real woman
I may be far from perfection
But I still deserve true dedication
I only fell in love with you
Because I saw you as my mirror reflection
We were one, I trusted you with my heart
You were my king and protection
But the only thing I needed saving from, was your rejection
So I thank you for the mental stimulation
To find the love of myself
And forcing me into the meditation
So I could see
That no matter the pain you brought into my life
It didn't kill me

Lesson Learned

What was the lesson learned?
I thought to myself
It all came back
To my lack of self-respect
Without respect there is no love
Trying to remember all the mistakes I could think of
That I had made in life that far
Since the day my family fell apart
I was reaching for love anywhere I could
From family to friends to men
Not taking the precautions I knew that I should
Just to end up the same
With things still not going my way
Sometimes I looked into the clouds
Just hoping for a sound
That would answer my prayers
Just to feel love
From the emotional issues
To the tribulations I was going through
I just wanted to scream
Just because I was comfortable in my skin
It does not mean
I was acceptable within
The real remedy was not with family or friends
The love I needed was not from men
I needed a real grasp on life
If I ever wanted to be someone's wife
Be successful and happy
Live in a world without strife
I needed to get to know me
Become my own best friend

To keep away from my enemy
This was myself
I was becoming my own personal bully
Using the physical control
That I was once told
Women can have over a man
To satisfy the loneliness
I was facing
Since the day my dad left me alone
I could not change the past
So I needed to accept all that
But make a change for the better
When I lost hope in my family
I depended on the world for guidance
Becoming lost to reality
I did not want to face the actualities
Even though I had so much more to learn
So much more to go through
I was learning respect was not given but earned
If I focused on that
Love would follow suit
In this phase everyone felt that I changed
But I was still me
Just my outlooks were not the same
My friends continued without my presence
I did not mind
They did not know my lessons
I kept dating but nothing too serious
In tunnel vision
I started to become more imperious
Taking control of my decisions
I no longer wanted to be promiscuous
So I returned to my written therapy
It was time to wind down

Gaining more clarity
The kind I needed being near my mid-twenties now

The way I felt...

If I become emotionally weak
He will be gone before a week
If I give it to him easy
He will be gone before the morning breeze
He will have no interest
Not knowing there are so many
Causes to the damage

I never wanted to be that woman
In that category
Or percentile
I never wanted to be included with that world
Known as living fast
Or living wild

I stick to my guns when it matters most
I wear my heart on my sleeve
I can never just let it coast
I always need to know
If you respect me or love me
Because I have no time to wait
To end up finding myself empty

I never wanted to be that woman
In that category
Or percentile
I never wanted to be included with that world
Known as living fast
Or living wild

I see the light
That it's not all bad men
I am being treated like the woman I act like

Love is blind to that physical make
Of the image my eyes create
I deserve more than minimal intentions
I recognize all the good
But the most important details I fail to pay attention

I never wanted to be that woman
In that category
Or percentile
I never wanted to be included with that world
Known as living fast
Or living wild

My brother always tells me
I am young and can't see
That different types of women
Do different types of things
Statistics have many bad ways
Like looking for love in wrong places
With none within

I never wanted to be that woman
In that category
Or percentile
I never wanted to be included with that world
Known as living fast
Or living wild

I stay
As if I don't believe I can find any better
He realizes this vendetta
I suffer from
So until I get enough
He will treat me like the woman I act like
Until I say

I AM NO LONGER THAT WOMAN

I never wanted to be that woman
In that category
Or percentile
I never wanted to be included with that world
Known as living fast
Or living wild

Now that I am older
I realize I needed certain situations
The bad has made me choose the good
As I change my mind's location
Just because I made mistakes
Does not make me a product of circumstance
The lessons that I learned were only there to enhance

I will never be that woman
In that category
Or percentile
I will never be included with that world
Known as living fast
Or living wild

SELF
RESPONSIBILITY

The way I felt...

I know I may want love
It is what I have always dreamed of
But not as bad as to corrupt myself
Continue to put my dignity on a shelf
While I search high and low for love
The fact that I have not found love
It seems the more I am willing to go through
Just to have love
Due to the choices
That love have given
It has left me feeling worthless
But I am the one at fault
Neglecting the values and morals
My mother has taught
By focusing my life on how to serve
Love to make me happy
Being without what I deserve
Just to feel its entirety
But it has caused a void in my heart
While creating bad decisions for my body
Overpowering the guidance from my soul
Making my confidence become rocky
Love have become toxic to my well being
It feels so good to have love
And that keeps me from seeing
Things that I need to
I only recognize the best in love
Blind myself from seeing the rest in love
Then the fool in me starts to take over
Every time that love appears
I become captivated in its arrival
When it should be feared
Not sure what each situation will entitle

I convince myself it is worth every battle
Of being brought up, just to be let down
By the pain and humiliation of heartache
Because after I see the top from the ground
Up is the only way from that place
Hoping the new knowledge I have found
Will prevent the next problem at that phase
Because falling down
Sometimes is better than it may feel
I realize this once the pain has all healed
And the lessons have been learned
As each page of life is turned
Hoping one day I will believe
It is worth to have loved and lost
Rather than never have loved at all
There are still things I do not understand
And many ways around it I wish I knew of
But all I know now is
I am unconscious to this thing called love

Looking for Love in Wrong Places

As many men came and went
The pure heart I truly had was recognized
As they missed the time that was spent
I was too busy being involved in self
I was not trying to hear any of their content
I believe someone has really lived life
Once they've been hurt by the one's they'll never forget
It is the joy and pain life brings
I wished I could be happy and content
With more material things
Instead of the abstract
Every time I felt that I was ready for change
Love came and threw me off track
I was enjoying life and focusing on me
When I finally accepted my friend's offer on a night out
What harm could be in one evening?
Plus, I could really use a release
So when the night came
I began getting ready
Then I was on my way
We finally arrived at some nightclub
As the music filled the room
And each drink filled my womb
The less I remembered my rules
One of my friends pulled me to the dance floor
The two of us immediately went to four
As these two men joined our movements
My friend and I continued to dance
The effects of the alcohol had me in some kind of trance
Until the music changed
And we decided to go back to our booth

Followed by these men that seemed a little strange
But after great conversation
Our contact information was exchanged
That was when I began to feel flutters in my stomach
It was all happening so sudden
Just when I promised myself to be solo
Love was trying to sneak back into my picture
I knew my guard was too high
To fall for just any type of guy
Then my heart fought my intuition
This had me thinking
That maybe he was different
So I ended up deciding to see how things went
I would not say that he was perfect
But it was different than I expected
It was the way he understood me
Our time together went so smoothly
We had no rush in what we were doing
He showed the most empathy
We shared our darkest secrets
I began really feeling he was the one

The way I felt...

Like being caught in an ocean's wave
I flow with your current
Every time I visualize
Looking into your forgiving eyes
I instantly become paralyzed
Like being bitten by a poisonous serpent
Sometimes it takes so much heartache and pain
Just to receive true happiness
Even though I do not expect any sympathy
I do appreciate all of your empathy
You broaden my horizons
In many ways you have enhanced me
All my burdens you have held as your own
You give me butterflies that flutter through my soul
Once I am in your arms, I regain my strength
Just to become weak as love takes control
It is truly unexplainable
I know there are many that question
What we see in one another?
But that is what makes our connection rare
We truly see each other
With the bond that we have
There are no obstacles we cannot defeat
I think I am in love
As you hold the last piece
To making my puzzle complete
My heart
It is so amazing
God brought me you
This is why I consider you such a blessing
So I make sure each night to thank Him
For taking the time to create you for me
All of this feels so crazy

Like when you compliment me
I feel like a super star
Beyond any fame or jewels
Just the one that is in your heart
That is why I cherish you holding me
Because you take me to this destination
I have never been before
And when we are together
I feel myself loving you more and more
I just need to know if I really have you

It Never Fails

That was when I realized
I could not control love
I could only be a part of it
So now that love was not the issue
I was ready for a world of new
Now it was my friends
That was becoming loose ends
They grouped together
Then turned on me
The night life was too tempting
But my invites became less
I was changing I will confess
We went from bonds full of trust
To being so out of touch
The hardest part
Of facing it all
When I needed them most
They deserted me
It seemed that everyone that was hurting me
Expressed their lack of emotion overtly
All I could do is think to myself
Where was their loyalty?

The way I felt...

Loyalty is a commitment of trust
Relationship or friendship
Even within family is a must

It is so easily broken
Twice as hard to rebuild
The lack of loyalty
Has been reason people kill

The reason friendships fall
Some think it is not that serious
Or not of importance at all

Learn the significance of honor
The honor you hold when one keeps their word
Not to mention the abundance of respect
This one word gives to the beholder

However

Temptation has made it so easy to betray
Fictitious behavior
Gives the disloyal away

As it exposes the guiltiness
The denial makes it worse
From whom it manifests
You must make the admittance step first

For lacking the dedication
To another that you claim to love
Loyalty is like the medication
To the problems that separations are made of

Some don't know how
To be loyal to someone else
Before you can judge another's loyalty
You must first take a look inside
At the loyalty in yourself

No New Friends

I admit I was being to myself
Especially having that new guy I was dating
But I always needed my friends
They were the ones that helped with my escaping
I guess with time comes change
I was willing to accept that
With my family abandonment, it was all the same
I never had a hard time meeting new people
This was exactly what I did
But I should have known that it was all too simple
I immediately became involved in a new group of women
Who introduced me to a new type of sinning
In their minds
The men with the most money were the ones winning
Their love I guess
Even though I was involved with my guy
I was anxious to see life from their side
Ever since my new man had broken my barrier
That I created to protect me
Now I was vulnerable to things much scarier
So as he became busy
I did not want to be a nag
So I decided to get a life outside of him
But once again, I was naive to all the red flags
I watched these women boast
About how they constantly popped tags
Buying all the expensive things
Was the way a man showed the love he had
Every night with them was like a movie
Flashing lights
V.I.P. nights

Not a worry in sight
Besides the senseless fights
In their minds
They had it all together
They were out in all kinds of weather
It did not matter
As long as money was flowing
And the marijuana was blowing
With liquor still pouring
It was a beautiful night
In their world
This was living the life

The way I felt...

You will sell your soul
For all the fancy in the world
High price clothes
Shoes, bags
You would even sale a touch of your pearl
It becomes so sad
Hundreds of dollars on weaves
Picassos on nails
Fluctuating men through your sheets
It is becoming so bad
You cannot even tell
Money is your addiction
Like a drug
You've become addicted to a life
That you have not worked for
Or deserve, therefore
You let yourself be used by the ballers
And the few
Married men with six digit careers
That you also give your body to
So they give you diamond rings
All the beautiful material things
But no love, no respect
For you, my material queen
You survive off this image you have created
Lord only knows if it ever gets outdated
It feeds your kids and pays your bills
Thinking life is a game
Having no jobs, no skills
This is all that you know
Addicted to makeup and retail
Your true beauty cannot show
This must stem from self-esteem issues

Girl wake up
Invest meaning in yourself
Instead of the gold-digging club
Before you have nothing left
My material queen
You are so much more
Than what is defined
The lies and the scandal
Brings problems that are harder to handle
Find your happiness within
My queen
Follow your dreams

A Different World

While they were living this life
They were all being blinded
So what was the price of one's sight?
These women wanted to have their own
They were inspired
To have self-worth and be independent
But the expectation of their environment
Subjected them to tradition
Creating these women to be vicious
Because the men were too busy being victims
I hated to see the hurt and pain
As it all surrounded me
The way my people expressed themselves
Killing each other's families
I was open to the distinct differences
Between their environment and mine
Following that experience
I started to appreciate the reasons
My mother was before running out of time
When she moved us away
To save my brothers from the temptations
Of a life full of crime

The way I felt...

The block is hot, the block is hot
Many calls and warnings at the sight of the cops

Death surrounds us
It's so hard to sleep
Sleepless nights, meatless meals
Trying to survive, and not become a victim of the streets
A victim to the creeps, a victim of defeat
Trying hard to maintain, selling drugs can be arranged
Other choices like school and jobs
To some sounds insane
Impossible at most
The more knowledge I try to soak
The more it feels I'm trying to boast
Their environment has raised them into being weak-minded
Weak hearts, weak souls

The block is hot, the block is hot
Many calls and warnings at the sight of the cops

I know he says he loves you
Like he loved that girl around the corner
He has one motive in mind
To be your next sperm donor
I understand no one has been there
So you believe the one that acts like they care
How could anyone love you?
When you do not love yourself
You push everyone away
And now there's nothing left
That's what you are used to
That's all you have ever been through
Every day you wake up

You are given a second chance
It's up to you to stand up
And truly understand
You're beautiful
So focus on being a better woman

The block is hot, the block is hot
Many calls and warnings at the sight of the cops

"There's no way out"
That is your excuse
The bottom line
Is you are indirectly caged through your mind
You have become an animal in this habitat
They built as projects
To control the generations, they call rejects
So why not strive to be better?
Do you want to survive this weather?
You have loved ones depending on you
So stand proud with your scarlet letter
We all carry our own
Because no one is perfect
No man's plan for you is written in stone
Unless you make it
People fought for your limitless opportunity
It's up to you to take it
Instead of fighting over a territory
Better yourself to become a role model
Put down the guns, drugs and liquor bottles
Then imagine your life
As alive and mentally free

The block is hot, the block is hot
Many calls and warnings at the sight of the cops

Friends vs. Foes

I wanted to empower these women
So I thought of a way I could help
To change their minds into the same of mine
Share the lessons I learned in the self-respect concept
They would always pay attention
This told me they were tired of settling
But their minds had run out of ammunition
Too tired of trying
So they ran out of ambition
Became captured in their ways
As they used drugs and alcohol to escape
The reality they were stuck in
As I thought I was being a true friend
By giving them other options to vent
And showing them the world I was in
It did not make sense to them
So they became angry with me
Unknowingly
I pulled and I pulled
Reaching my hand to these women
All this time I thought we were in it together
They were convincing themselves
That I believed I was better
Because they thought I was
So I instantly
Became their enemy
Target of their party of pity
It was all Satan's work
He was really trying to get me
Working through the weak
Because I was too guarded in prayer

I do admit
He almost reached my deepest layer
He had these women ready
To bring pain and hurt upon me
Just to make me angry
So I would join his team
As he knew revenge would be in me
I still sometimes send thanks to God
Because he protected me
Against all odds

The way I felt...

With a friend like you
Who needs enemies?
Had no good intentions
Since the day you befriended me
Silly me
But no judgments passed
On my behalf at least
I am tired of your judgments
See I may have been naive
I will accept my responsibility
Like believing that we are equal
Accepting your disloyalty
You are a tainted being
Taking advantage of my reality
To use for your own meaning
You laugh now
As your thrills are based on my misery
You must understand
There will be a day
Your skies will become gray
Then you will think back to your disgraceful ways
Become ashamed
Wish to apologize for your selfish days
I used to question your mischievous behavior
The excuses I imagined your tongue will bear
Made me decide it's better to not care
It is bad enough that you are cutting your own blessings
Amazing that you have not learned your lessons
Especially when your life consists of many bad situations
Now you are mad
Frustrated
Because that whirlwind of unexplained
Has non-verbally stated

The many things you shouldn't have done
I know facing the problems can be hard
Getting through them is critical
But releasing your negative energy onto me
Only makes me more cynical
Of you
All the gossiping and jealousy
Seem to be the only traits you portray
So from this moment I steer clear of you
Because real will not tolerate fake
I want to just wait
For my time to retaliate
And not even hesitate
But I will be going against my better judgment
To prove a point to ones not worth it
So the best way I serve it
With confidence
That seems to hit the hardest
The way I continue with kindness
Just know the friendship is behind us
There is no sense in asking why
It will be left unanswered
The art of my inner peace
I have been forced to master
You are the one that is truly weak-minded
Because you block the love, trust and care
To continue being blinded
Even as the victim
I also have fault
Because I have constantly let some
Of the same type of people in
While expecting a different outcome

Circles

Back to my current relationship
At least that was still going good
He held my hand through the recent madness
Doing everything he could
To bring light to my life
Until one night out of the blue
He sent me an address to come to
When I arrived it was a beautiful summer night
We were right off the water
Not a person in sight
Just us
He held me from behind
As I stood in front of him
He asked what was on my mind
So I decided to tell him
That I had been feeling his distance
He told me he loved me
Right before I met the new friends
And it had not been the same since
I tried to understand work complications
That had made him so busy
Plus, I had those problems in my life I was facing
I just needed some honesty
Or should I say reassurance
After all the madness with family and friends
I did not know who to trust
He began to cry
Saying since his father passed he felt out of touch
He looked to the sky
Then back down into my eyes
Told me that everything had been too much

He needed a break
I asked, what did he mean?
Was he referring to me?
And he nodded his head
As he began to plead
That I do not walk out of his life completely
I was frozen in time
It was a mixture of emotion
Heartache and anger
I needed this man
He was the only breath of fresh air
I had left
Or was he

The way I felt...

Once upon a time I loved you too much
I really didn't even care if I was used as a crutch
Or if you just liked the feel of my touch
Either way I wanted you
Any way that I could have you
Anything it took for me to do
Any obstacle course you took me through
I did it with ease
Don't say you don't love me back
Don't you dare get on that track
Learn to love me I will wait
Say I do, with the vows we take
For heaven's sake
You were made for me
This was our destiny
It went from a dream to epiphany
Your presence
Inspired my heartbeats to play a symphony
You were the director
But in a whole different sector
Your heart is not with mine
Blinded by speeding time
Scared of the post- goodbye
Of what your life may be like
So you stayed with me
That was unfair to my intentions
The one-sided love you didn't mention
So I kept on playing this position
Making a complete fool of myself
Now you are all apologetic
That don't change how pathetic
I feel right now
Thinking you're saving me with amends

Talking about let's be good friends
I have had enough of your pretend
To care for me
Try being there for me
Put yourself in my shoes
Stop living safe, because you are scared to lose
Be honest
I do not know who you really are
And I may not ever know

To Be or Not To Be

So now heartbroken and full of tears
I was back to being alone
This place was becoming familiar
I learned before I was never on my own
But even though God was by my side
I was still lonely in this flesh
I could not stop the tears I cried
Nor the pain that dwelled inside
I began to miss my real friends
They were the only ones
I felt could relate to the pain I was in
I wanted to forgive them
Just to have them back in my life
So I called and left voicemails
Just to give my apologies one night
To no surprise, no answer
As they were probably together
Enjoying some type of night life
I realized the part I played
In why our friendships started to fade
It was not the fact that they changed
We were all at a developing age
That's when my thoughts were broken
As my phone began to ring
It was my ex
I did not know if I should answer
Because I knew there was a catch
I answered to him giving plenty of excuses
Then offered something way more farfetched
He had a trip coming up for work
He invited me to come along

In hopes we could have time away to talk
But I was getting tired of his same sad song
Going back and forth
Not knowing what it is he wanted
But with family being out of the picture
And my friendships still needing fixing
Maybe a vacation was exactly what I needed
So I accepted
Once we arrived to our destination
He instantly began acting like that night did not happen
He was trying to ignore my hesitation
But we had to talk about his actions
The instant heartbreak had stolen my passion
For him

The way I felt...

I twist and I turn
Not knowing which way to run
So I feel stuck
Like I am running in place
Straining every muscle within
Too captured in my feelings
Without a thought to lend
Am I really this hopeless?
Can I make it out of this box?
My mind is depending on a solution to come
When all along I hold the key to the lock
That is placed inside my heart
I must not be seeing the bigger picture
That keeps overwhelming me
I cannot see the forest for looking at the trees
Blinding myself when it could all be so simple
I am just so wrapped up in finding nothing
That all the simple seems unreal
But the lessons learned
Would not stick for a reason or another
Because the end results
Would be someone making me suffer
Or am I doing this to myself?
Should I do what makes me happy?
Or what makes sense to me in each situation?
Without thinking ahead
I will never realize the constant replications
Over and over again
I will face the same battles
Breaking more barriers of my skin
That is no longer as thick as it once was
I am not as strong as I once was
I have broken myself one time too many

When will I ever get tired?
Of looking for that big epiphany
That revelation that I dream would come
As long as the lessons are not being learned
To this recurring misery
I will continue to succumb
So I shall restart this journey again
Picking up the pieces of my heart and spirit
That was broken from the last time
Now I will look for it
So it cannot sneak into my way
Then maybe I will stop making four lefts
That brings me back to point A

Damaged Me

I was getting pains in my abdomen
For the past two weeks
I had been in and out of the hospital
And my body was becoming physically weak
That was when I realized
I was putting my health at risk
Just to have this thing called love
That I was too prideful to admit
With all the tests the doctor ran
I was scared to death
Then finally the doctor came in
With his clipboard in hard
Advising my eating had to get better
My stress needed more control
Then he handed me a letter
Explaining a surgery I had to undergo
But it was just one obstacle
The doctor advised we must get through
Based on the results
He said, "There is a baby inside of you"
He followed with the urgency
Of getting this well-needed surgery
Because the issues I was having
At some point it could have killed me
Since the pregnancy was only estimated at 8 weeks
There was a high chance
The surgery could cause defects to the baby
So I was stuck in an emotional trance
I figured this vacation was perfect
I could tell my ex everything
While we were away

So we finally arrived
At the vacation place
One night we were out to dinner
Scheduled to leave the next day
I decided to tell him the news
But before I could say it
He said he had something to tell me too
I allowed him to go first
He went on about being honest
Saying besides losing his dad
He had a secret he was holding for the longest
He had been scared to tell me
Because he knew I was already guarded
Saying he needed to be open, as he always promised
His ex was still in his life
There were feelings for her that he could no longer fight
Just when I thought the pain couldn't get any worse
Here I was with this man
That was still in love with the woman he had first
Of course I decided at that moment to keep my secret
For the next two hours he constantly pleaded
To get the information out of me
I was now twice as angry
I promised myself that night to never trust another man
I was officially damaged
I just couldn't understand

The way I felt...

Sitting by myself thinking
How did you do this?
Made such a huge fool of me
The master of heart's trickery
In the beginning you were so perfect
Or maybe I was so stupid
Either way I fell under your spell
Now I cannot even tell
Left from right
My brain is so tight
I squeeze my eyes closed
Hoping I wake in a new life
You damaged me

If only I could become you for one hour
I would destroy your reputation
Strip away all of your power
Take away that immaculate smile
Your heart I would devour
I am so tired of being hurt by you
So sick of your excuses
The unnecessary pain you put me through
You Damaged Me

You took me for granted
When I only wanted to love you
At one point you controlled me
As your existence completely
Took me over and drained me slowly
As your lies was steady flowing
Down to this very moment
Claiming that you love me
You Damaged Me

Your selfish standing ways
That will not go away
No matter how many times
I forgive you and your lines
Of untrue and deceit
Of hurt and misleading
I am fighting for no reason
Trying to change you and your mind
Instead of realizing
What I deserve from what is truly mine
You damaged me

I keep beating up myself
For allowing you to use me
Until nothing was left
Not realizing besides losing you
I will be losing myself
You leave and come back
I walk right into your next attack
You damaged me

I wish I could grow the voice to speak to you
Instead
I become weak
Can't think, can't speak
Can't breathe, can't see
How do you hold this control?
To prevent me from letting go
You damaged me

You weaken my spirit
Then my heart makes decisions
My mind with better judgments
Is ignored with your distorted visions

You paint with your "bigger pictures"
When really you are against us
This storm you brought into my life
Have hailed on my happiness
Struck lightning through my heart
Brought pouring tears to my eyes
You damaged me

I tried to forgive you
Thinking it was easier to pretend
I am too full of resentment
To ever trust again
So I pray
The sun will shine again
It cannot now with you in its way
Moving on from you is a must
In order to regain solid love and trust
Within my own
I can no longer let you damage me
You have had your way, way too long

Gone Forever

I ended up leaving that night instead
I needed to travel back alone
It was the only way to clear my head
I had to make the decision on my own
To either have that surgery and take the chance
Or risk my life to have our child
It was by far the hardest circumstance
Eventually I decided to have the surgery
As the pain began to get unbearable
I lost over 70 pounds, unable to eat
Three weeks later, there I was
Laying in my mother's home
As thoughts of raising this child on my own
Began to take over my brain
I concluded it was only fair to tell him the truth
Despite my heart's pain
It was the right thing to do
I explained the situation
He immediately started with his dictations
Trying to demand the child was carried to term
I made it clear
That it may have been his sperm
But it is my body I strongly affirmed
Then he hung up the phone right in my ear
That was when I allowed that one last tear
I would ever allow him to dwell in my eyes

The way I felt...

All the lying and the crying that we went through
You will miss it twice as much as I miss you
You will miss the sound of my sorrows
The love
That will not come tomorrow
Because you left me in the cold alone
You had me feeling ashamed and down
Eventually my dignity was found
I was vulnerable trying to feel wanted and worthy
When you made the vision of our future so blurry
By always making me feel like I'm in some race
And I was playing myself
Because I knew
I was always worth first place
To anyone deserving
I was too strong for you
And instead of becoming stronger
You made me your number two
When it came to your heart
So bringing it back to the current
The way I'm saying goodbye
I want the most painful way to interpret
To break your heart with every line
Because I feel like a Gemini
With these different emotions inside
One day I can't stand you
The next day I can't live without you
I do not want that anymore
I'm done with the hurt that I store
I don't know how you want me to act
I don't know what you want me to say
I begged you not to do me like that

So, in hell there will be a cold day
Before I ever trust or give my all again
I don't know who I was
But I know who I am now
In the mode of me, myself and I
The three you left me with
My ego matches yours
I walk with a stride
Taking my eyes off the ground
Putting my head to the sky
And the tears you see constantly
Dropping from my eyes
Like it does from the skies
When God cries with me
They are just my feelings being released
I have accepted the relationship is gone
All the love, was good while it lasted
So if a friendship is restored
Hopefully it can out last it
I always say I'll never get back with you
And I was warned never say never
So on that note
I would just say that the "us" is gone forever

At Last

I decided to get an abortion
I was not ready to bring a new life into this world
My life was already full of distortion
But I lost sight of my faith at that moment
I knew God would have never blessed me with that child
If it was not what he wanted
Or a part of his plan
There I was a week later
In the waiting room of Planned Parenthood
At first I did not realize what I was deciding to do
I may have known about the procedure
But not the aftermath I would go through
I was so caught in my own selfish feelings
I did not think of the life I was taking away
Once it was all over
I fell into a ball of confusion
Because I ended up suffering either way
In the beginning thinking of others before myself
Felt like punishment
Now thinking of myself first
Was even more punishing
I felt like my life was one big curse
I was ready to surrender
I fell to my knees with my arms stretched out
With my heart so tender
I needed God's arrival
So I fell into deep prayer, repentance and revival

The way I felt...

No words can explain
No excuse is enough
Even though my mind changed
Because my life got tough
I gave up on you
I was not ready to raise you
Sometimes I wish I could go back and save you
Instead I gave you
Up
It hurts to reminisce
Of the weeks we shared
The disconnection I feared
But still I gave you
Up
I know God is now with you
He will protect you
From anything that's against you
Hopefully, one day I will meet you
Until then I will just miss you
Who you would have become
I try not to think of
Some nights I tear up
At my decision
That I must live with
So I just pray
This is my only way
To talk to you
I hope that you forgive me
As I know God has
I wrote this letter to get it all off my chest
And let my soul be at peace
At last

HAPPINESS IN SELF

The way I felt...

There is no way to succeed
If I lose the hunger
Fighting through the challenges
Convinced it is making me stronger
When I have run out of options
My mind becomes blank
As a fresh sheet of my journal
Before I let my ink flow and release my internal
Pain, as my brain and heart starts to rumble
Ideas and hope start to develop
Then I implement
Letting God be my guide

I know I cannot trust anyone but myself
Only I know my heights
They are beyond the clouds
Only I see my visions
That I believe the Lord has endowed
So I keep searching
I am like a forest fire in the middle of July
Unable to be stopped

As I think of the tears I have cried
The hard times
Loose ends, that remains untied
Memories I hold inside
Had no one around to confide
The devil kept trying to enter my life
But I would not let him

I am beginning to feel alone in this moment
Because I will not allow my happiness to be stolen
Or maybe it is because of my accomplishments

Or that I move with prominence
And never allow the world to control my confidence
After all the heartbreaks over nonsense

I am uncomfortable with having nothing
Though I am grateful for the days I wake up
And the blessings that keep coming
This is not the peak of my purpose
There is no sense in feeling pointless
Thinking certain things matter when they don't
It all drowns me like a toxic-filled substance

Sometimes I think of the place I will feel content
When everything will make sense
I will have everything I believe I deserve
And I can finally stop feeling so tense
Then I will realize that I was everything I strived not to be
Letting the judgments of the world motivate me
When actually
The true meaning of my movements will be lost
Until my heart and my spirit meets in one place
But until then
I will never be content

Life is Short

It was two years later
When I came out of my shell
And back to my right mind
Back focused on ways to excel
Plus, following that revelation
I was more thoughtful of situations
I was putting myself in
My world was all about me
I started to believe
In the worth of myself that I fought for daily
I was just happy that I finally realized this
Before I really went crazy
But it found me like a court summons
All of it built the woman I was becoming
I was eventually able to get my friends back
After they made me sit through hours of attacks
On their feelings of how my side of the friendship had slacked
But I did not mind
They helped me realize things within myself
Like breaking the rule of being the friend that never left
Then on the other end of my life
My family helped me pull myself together
Everyone was focusing on their own endeavors
But they were still right by my side
And that made our love stronger than ever
Looking back at it all
The biggest lesson I learned through my falls
Was life being too short to be unhappy
Or surround myself with misery
I had so much to be thankful for
To be dwelling on bad memories

So it was time to leave the negativity
To stay buried in my written therapy
Besides my friends and family that helped
I had another life-changing experience
That contributed to the way I felt
It was so hard to accept
The loss of my grandmother
With only faded memories that were kept
Because I did not see her as often as I should
Due to her lack of her presence in my childhood
Her and my mother's independence
Both contributed to my journey to womanhood
My grandmother's survival
Of abuse and single-motherhood
Ignited the fire I needed within myself
But, it made it hard for her to trust
So she became an antagonist to everyone else
She was still one of my heroes
All that she had been through
Reassured me I could keep fighting too
But the part that always made me a mess
Was trying to accept that she was gone in the flesh
I tried to remember she was protecting me from above
And was able to see parts of me
She did not see when she was with us
The best part of this truth
I knew she would see
That I was more like her than she ever knew

The way I felt...

The silence holds me
Because I am lost without words
As the memories are told
Of the strength you unfold
Created by your struggle
So undeserved to your being
There is no more
You have conquered the real war
Of this journey called life
You are a true soldier

Though you left without a sound
Your presence still feels loud
Louder than a Martin's speech
You hold the strength of an army
With enough wisdom to move mountains
You always shared knowledge
Despite all the worldly pressure
You were always so put together

I know I will miss your flesh
Even as a misunderstood presence
It used to feel
You put one's patience to a test
But amazingly you were bringing out the best
Of anyone blessed to know you
And the way you spoke your truth
No filter was needed
That is how most of your lectures succeeded

Now I am scared of this death
As you are not here
Seeing your flesh without a soul

Not knowing how it took your last breath
Or what holds your existence
When I see the legacy you left
As we each holds different parts of you
I refrain from feeling any hurt
Because when I last saw your lifeless body
As you were lowered back to the earth
The cries that surrounded
Made it all hit me
I realized my day would come

The lesson I learned
Life is not an option
So as you dawn from above
And watch us take it all for granted
Exchanging hate instead of love
You must help me
With the strength to fight the negativity

I pray you will rest in peace
I know you will protect me
So as the clouds moved aside
And God shined his light
He brought home an angel
That is now a guardian angel of mine

Maturing Mindset

Losing loved ones was a part of growing up
It helps appreciate the loved ones still with you
As I watched my dad fall apart for the second time in my life
Due to the death of his mother
I knew I needed to be the strength
For us to get through this hard time
So I became more determined to accomplish my goals
I knew the next time my family needed me
I could not fall as before and just fold
And that is when it happened to me
It was amazing
I was blessed with two little sisters
Like angels that just fell from the sky
They needed me more than ever
I knew God was giving me a sign
That it was time to stop all my cries
Put my strength into overdrive
I was now an influence for two new lives
It seemed that time flew by
One moment they were fresh out of the hospital
Then were tall enough to stare into my eyes
They were exactly what I needed
Bloodline or not
As they loved me unconditionally
From the first moment we made contact
They became my family instantly
Once they were here
I could not live my life without them
They are the pillars to my life
They keep me grounded
Mentally and emotionally

The way their light shined so bright
And just the thought of their struggle
I could not imagine their fight
So I just prayed for God
To help me show them what a real woman is like

The way I felt...

Delicate as a flower
Reaching for life's knowledge
This cruel world's blessing
Yet it does not even acknowledge
The gift God has made
With the strength you endure
With your hearts so pure
It is beyond any extreme
That I could ever think I will fear
You have defeated the abuse
From substances, before you had life
This makes you amazing in your own little way
And it leaves me trying to be perfect for you
So when your mind becomes that troubled maze
Hopefully I can protect you
Be there for you always
Nothing can come between
Our treasured moments
Even when you grow older
And try to disown it
Like the times you feel I embarrass you
When I force you to take responsibility
For wrong-doing you decide to do
It always has a purpose
Know that I only want the best for you
You are now parts of me
And sometimes it makes me feel nervous
Because as you look upon me for direction
I want your minds and hearts to be nourished
With values and morals most fruitful
I want you knowledgeable of what you may go through
If anything comes to try and hurt you
You can protect yourself

God works in mysterious ways
So I teach you in every way
That I can, to give you a better start
So you will always have an open heart
To receive when God talks to you
I want you to know how wonderful you are
And the way you filled the voids in my heart
You were right on time
To put breath back into me
When I did not have any
Inhales left to give myself
I am forever indebted to you
When God brought me you
You became the wind beneath my wings
That I needed to fly again
And for my new life decisions to begin
Whenever I look at either of you
I thank the Lord for seeing
Exactly what I needed
And I thank you for being
My solution to being treated
So I want you to witness
That anything you aspire to be in life
Is not impossible
Because with true openness
No matter the distance of your dreams
Your opportunities are limitless

My King

I could not ask for anything else
I felt so free and clear
I was in love with myself
I believe every woman needs that time
To be alone and have a stable and clear mind
That was when it happened again
I ended up meeting this guy
But that was what made love worth it
When you try time after time
This situation was different
I had known this man most of my life
We grew up together
As a young girl I was mesmerized
But he never looked at me twice
Now that we were grown
I had developed into my own
I had finally caught his eye
There were times
It felt like a fairytale
Just when I thought
Finding true love was unreal
He changed my mind
He asked me to believe and confide
Try to set my prior experiences aside
To give something real, a genuine try
Even though I felt
My hope for love had died
Something within
Made me consider what he implied
It was the best decision
I had made in a very long time

With all the joys and pains I had been through
It was breath-taking
To finally have love that was mutual
The way his strength matched mine
It opened my eyes
It was weak men
I allowed in my past
That was intimidated by strong women
He continued to show me what true love was
I slowly regained belief that true love existed
So even though
It felt like it all happened so suddenly
I could see this man one day as my husband
And thanked God
To have him by my side in the end
It was amazing
To have a lover in a best friend

The way I felt...

There are so many things I want to tell you
No secrets between you and me
I want you to know me from my core
Down to my deepest layers
My most powerful treasures
Where you can learn how to love me
See, I have this image of what I wanted you to be
But since you have found me
The things I thought I wanted in you
Have now become so minimal
Compared to what I truly need
I believe our love will be power
The way you grasp the world with one hand
Holding my heart with the other
You make me want to take the chance
Of anything I want to discover
So moving mountains will be light as a feather
As the strength of our love grows
We will bring sunshine to other's stormy weather
We will give the aching hearts hope
The ones with damaged hearts a remedy
I know this may sound ridiculous
But it is amazing when your blessings
Can result in another person's gain
I used to dream of this moment
I know every little girl wants it
The time you can exhale
Release all the bad memories
Forget the past of the ones before
Start a brand new journey
Our love will start our own bloodline
Blessed with life lessons only to keep learning
We will build a solid foundation

And like the leaves on the trees
I will flow with your breeze
As you devour my fears
Place water upon my seeds
I will grow with you
So I need your knowledge
To guide me through
I am letting go of all the burdens
So we can move forward
Sometimes I can become a lot of work
My emotions will climb high
That is why I need your patience
You control them and help bring them back inside
I can lie here forever
And just stare into your eyes
We can let the entire cruel world
Stay outside
Here in our world
It can just be you and I
We can let ourselves go into each other
We will start the rest of our lives
Then continue on our journey together
With God as our guide

What is Love?

I did not realize how hard love could be
It always sounded magical
All my past relationships were just casual
There wasn't any substance
When there is no value in the love shared
It is just lust
I had become so reluctant
To opening up my heart to another
But this man was my adjustment
He knocked down the judgments
I had in production
Of dishonesty within men
My horizons were broadened
As I learned the true definition of love
This man was restoring my confidence
He broke down my dominance
Reminded me I am a woman
That deserves to be conscious
Of the way it feels to be acknowledged
So no matter how many years of college
Or how many defeated challenges
I could still be weak
The more time we were together
The more he gave my heart shelter
As he prayed with me
Catered to my sensitivity
Embraced my strengths
And prayed for me
I became convinced
That true love existed

The way I felt...

Love is patience
When you are present in my hardest moments
Then make them feel not as important

Love is not envy
As we each prosper through life
We will be joyous of each other's accomplishments

Love is kindness
Of sharing our hearts with each other
Giving more than taking

Love is not boasting
Blessings come on God's timing
As quickly as they are given, they can be taken

Love is not proud
As we express our emotions
No need to hide the joy or pain

Love is honor
Be the king of our castle
As your queen I am here to serve you

Love is selfless
Your needs become mine
We will become one from two

Love is happiness
You bring out of my soul
Teaching me to accept
What's not in my control

Love is forgiveness
Everyone makes mistakes
We will learn to let go

Love is truth
Keeping open communication
Letting honesty be its core

Love is hope
When I feel as though I have settled for less
You keep me focused on gaining so much more

Love is trust
I will follow your lead
Believe in your dreams as mine

Love is protection
With my life in your hands
I am secure with a peace of mind

Love is compassion
You surprise me with daily
You understand my flaws

Love is perseverance
Even when blessings do not come on our timing
You catch us when we are sure to fall

Love is knowledge
You have brought upon me
Showing me all the right things I have missed

Love is the ear
That you plant to my problems
Including mistakes I am afraid to admit

Love is conquering
Since our beginning we have sacrificed a lot
But we have always succeeded
Our limit is the sky

Love is, you and I

Open My Heart

I was in a great space
Mentally and emotionally
Thanks to my mother
The ways she always stepped in
And thanks to my brothers
They knew what to say and when
And thanks to that man
He walked into my life
At a very hard time
But the challenges I came with
Did not change his mind
He cherished me
At times he carried me
Showed me
What real love was
I was just grateful
For everything they all did
I was so worried about my falls
That I was holding myself back
Instead of focusing on the love that I lacked
I just needed to learn
To acknowledge the love that I had
So I was happy to have the ones I needed most
Back in my life
Now my only focus was to always keep them close

The way I felt...

I beg and I plead
Please just believe in me
I know it seems I flip and I flop
To find my way to the top
And at the times that I didn't know
I decided to just stop
Understand that I try
When both of my ends are tied
It feels like I put love and family to the side
It is because I have cried
From it being hard to accept
That I let the feelings of defeat intercept
Know I will always rise back to life
With a new vision from the smiles I sacrificed
That has now been re-planted by Christ
Which I give thanks to every chance I can
Bad or good
I know it was part of God's plan
We all we got!
The motto that got our family through a lot
Therefore, I will never forget where I come from
Nor the strength I am made of
I must continue to have this drive
That is bigger than just to survive
So, I beg and I plead
Please just believe in me
I admit it may seem
That I'm selfish to live my dreams
But it is so much more than that
To my lovely mother
I see what you deserve
It's beyond all the diamonds and pearls
It is to be able to travel around the world

And life without any turmoil
You have faced enough
Lived your life in this box
For far too long
I am forever grateful
But content, I am not
My brothers, you understand
You have always been my right hand men
You saw my struggle, felt my pain
Kept it true with me through loss and gain
I was never judged by you
After all the fights we have gone through
You remained true and faithful
Believed in me
When I did not believe in myself
You are my wealth
My father of flesh
You were my biggest test
Never let my heart rest
I grew from the agony
You created strength inside of me
Brought out a different side of me
No matter what trials you faced
You were always right beside me
You inspired me
Gave me knowledge of life
Even when it was not what I wanted to hear
You always shared honesty
Tried your best to keep my mind clear
When you could have just lied
I hold all of you as precious tokens
I am convinced our bonds will never be broken
No weapons formed against us shall prosper
Because it's by God's grace
That we made it through

All of life's speed bumps
I am ready to be at last with all of you
I apologize for the emotions that I hide
I am taking this moment to give my truth

Fix My Life

I remember the day like it was yesterday
It was a familiar feeling in a weird way
My body did not feel like usual
So there I was at some store
In a bathroom cubicle
Taking a pregnancy test
I was too nervous to wait
My anxiety at its best
As the second line appeared
I jumped up and down
Whispering my screaming cheer
It felt like God was giving me a second chance
To do what was right
With this blessing that only He grants
In one's life
After the first doctor's appointment made it official
I knew there was a new life inside of me
That was the moment I felt most blissful
Everything in my life was about to change
Starting with the things I had to throw away
See, in my darkest moments of life
I created some habits
As my way to face challenges
But now those addictions
That was once so powerful
Was overpowered
By a being more masterful

The way I felt...

Addiction
I have become addicted to your existence
Your highs have brought me out of my lows
The way you ease the tension
I hate that you end so soon
The times you give me better days
The way you make me feel better
You are my therapy and counseling in so many ways
Getting me through times I am ready to give up
Calming me down when I would go crazy
Through my trials that I face
Somehow it is like you save me
From falling off the cliff of sanity
But in reality
You are not what's best for me
I used to deny believing this
Because you are so bad
I must acknowledge the control you have
How you have captivated me?
With temporary relief
That always ends eventually
Throwing all my visions off their course
While I lose sight of future worth
While you cause health issues
That I am not aware of
So thankfully, I have come out of that darkness
Before it was too late
Gaining back the control I had once
In determining my own fate
So I am proud of my rise
Above the temptation of failure
No more hiding behind lies
Just to excuse not breaking the real barrier

Now I have truly broken free
With a mind of clarity
Though my struggles may be life long
My strength will develop elsewhere
My addiction is now long gone

Reunited

My unborn child was changing things
Before he or she started breathing
Like this most incredible experience
Of bringing two hearts back together
That was not in each other's existence
My mother and I
Even though she was always there
So was the hurt
From the times I felt she did not care
Once I decided to face this new journey
Going into motherhood
Her support
Expressed a true love was appearing
All the times I felt she did not listen
To my cries
It was more of my incoherence
That was interfering
So as a soon-to-be mother of my own
I was able to learn the words of her song
My unborn child helped me shine a new light
On a major missing piece of the puzzle in life
There I was asking for her forgiveness
So we could make up lost time
I had so much to make up to her
I thought in my mind
When I thought of this legacy that she had created
With my child as the third generation
I began to understand her struggle
I instantly began thanking God for her patience
For her dedication
For her affection

For her determination
She never gave up

The way I felt...

I promise
To spend the rest of my life serving you
There were times
I felt I didn't deserve you
As I watched the struggles
The world took you through
You stood with strength
That only God could have given you
We were not very close when I was young
This left me blinded
To the hurt that was being done
I did not know the facts to your way of life
It took many years
But I finally see your sacrifices
You are a strong black woman
It shows through your pride
Sometimes I see the pain
That dwells within, through your eyes
I wish I could take it away
So you only feel happiness inside
Leave the past in the past
Let those tears become dried
You nurture two lives
That another person created
A single mother that raised five by yourself
And we all made it
I know you made me the strong woman
That I stand as today
Even though there was no father
You made sure we had better days
Never let the world see you sweat
As you faced your mistakes
I am just blessed for the fact that you are here

Despite my selfish feelings
You stood right beside me
As you took away my fears
You gave me the knowledge of faith
You always took a stand
Educated me on God's work and word
You always held my hand
I appreciate you
Wouldn't be anywhere near where I am
Without you
You are my backbone that gives me posture
When life makes me fall handicapped
You do everything that God will allow you to
So I love you
You brought me into this life
Never giving up
Made me want my future just as bright
As your smile
When I place it upon your face
I am the creation you and God made
I was no mistake
And I am grateful for your faith
In me

Labor Pains

We were having a baby girl
I told her dad I was about to explode
As she was getting ready to approach this world
He was trying to keep everything under control
But I could tell he was in a mind of unknown
As we rushed to the hospital
And he pushed me to the labor department
Followed by my mother
Storming in like a sergeant
She began helping me through
Every time the contractions started
Until they finally gave me the epidural
Then all the pain was gone
I was on cloud nine
With the love of my life
And my mother by my side
I was ready to give birth
And meet my princess
We waited and waited
As my friends started to come
The nurse came to check me
She announced my pregnancy was done
Our baby girl was finally ready to meet us
Before I knew it I heard her cries
Sounding like a choir of angels
Until I looked into her eyes
At that moment I finally realized
There is a love so deep
That one could never describe
Everything I went through
Was worth it at this moment

It all built the strength in me
To become this imperfect woman

The way I felt...

I wish I could press pause
Stand still in these memories
Keep you safe within my arms
Stay planted in our chemistry
Since the day I gave birth to you
It's been the best moments ever
When I look into your eyes
I feel a breath of fresh air
Unconditional love
That only you and I share
You resemble my heart
The more I see your development
Every day you learn something new
When you show me I melt
The way you make me feel is indescribable
You are my inspiration
Through your smile
I hold my strength to survive
As the fruit of my womb
You nourish my soul
Teaching me patience
The thought of you
Comfort me through any situation
Your mind is always wanting for more
You take in all that you can
As you observe the world
I protect you from the wrong
And teach you the right
I can see a piece of your dad and me
In every part of you
Such the perfect creation
We both watch you grow and bloom
Fall more in love with you

There was a time I thought we were not ready
To raise and nurture you
I am so proud as we work together
I never thought we could be so selfless
But you have truly changed us for the better
You are really growing on me
Seems like yesterday you were born
And I carried you in one arm only
Now you are walking and speaking
Next you will be too grown for me
I remember your first words
Your first steps
I will never forget
The memories
You share with me
As I watch you grow into a woman
The light in your eyes tells me
You will be something
Someone of importance
This is the meaning of your name's origin
I don't even worry about me
As long as I have enough for you
I want to protect you
Take away all your future issues
Before they can even get a chance to reach you
I will not always agree with you
And vice versa
But when it happens
Right or wrong
I'll forever nurture your actions
I miss you whenever life pulls me away
I have to work, you have school
So I keep your photo with me each day
You are my strength and my weakness
But still my biggest blessing either way

Though I am excited to see
The masterpiece you will become
Your importance in this flesh
Is destined in the legacy you are from
Believe in this my angel
Your powerful journey has just begun
I knew the first day
I looked into your dark brown eyes
God blessed me with something special
It was no surprise
To find out that He sent you
As my in the flesh angel in disguise

Imperfect Angel

I was now a mother
It made the world seem different
As I reminisced in my mind
Of all my trying times
I knew it was time
To take control of my life
It was time to own it
I never imagined adulthood being so hard
Growing apart from friends
Learning to live without the negativity I discard
Because I felt so used to it
I had been living in it so long
I needed to learn to neglect it with my intuition
To know it was coming before I go through it
It was time for change
It was time to grow up
My life had to be rearranged
But it was for the better
After all that stormy weather
I finally had sunlight
After all I had overcome
The pain of my past was done
I realized I had so much life to live
I had so much love to give
I was thankful
I had the ones that matters the most
I had to see all the answers were within
Because once I loved my own skin
Inside and out
A whole new life began
I love my imperfections

That is what makes me human
I love my huge heart
It is how my blessings and I have union
Even though my life's path has not always been stable
I have always been true
Accepting the truth sometimes was the most painful
But it was the best awakening I had
When I realized that I am an imperfect angel